# The Accessories We Wear

# The Accessories We Wear

*Some accessories I chose ...*
*Some accessories chose me*

## DR. RADSCHEDA R. NOBLES

**Ordering Information:**

Orders by U.S. trade bookstores and wholesalers. Quantity sales: Special discounts are available on quantity purchases by corporations, associations, and others. For details, contact the publisher at the following email address:

**Connect with Dr. Radscheda R. Nobles:**

**Email:**
drradscheda@gmail.com

# Part I

*Healing isn't immediate. It takes time, and it is a messy process. Sometimes it's one step forward, two steps back. This book accurately depicts a woman trying to survive and accept her wounds, scars, failures, and victories . . . all of herself. However, survival is an ever-evolving process. There are some things that a person will discover during their survival journey that are more difficult to accept than others.*

**Boy, don't I know about this...**

# Author Bio

**Dr. Radscheda R. Nobles** was born in Greenville, North Carolina, and raised in Fayetteville, North Carolina. She received a Ph.D. in Sociology from Howard University, a Master's Degree in Criminal Justice from Fayetteville State University, a Bachelor's Degree in Criminal Justice from Shaw University, and a GED from Pitt Community College. Nowadays, she teaches at the university level and shares her life stories wherever the opportunities present themselves.

# Dedication

*I dedicate this book to my mama, who was a writer. Thank you for inspiring my love of writing. This book honors her memory.*

*I love you, and I am sorry.*

# Table of Contents



**Close the book and flip it over to read
Part II of my story**

# Preface

Only by telling my mama's story can I honestly tell mine. So, I decided to write this book to help heal the wounds that bind us together. Why? Because they are part of us. It has been challenging to decide what information to share and what not to share, whom it will affect, and how I will be perceived. I've made the decision just to tell my truth. This is not my struggle alone; many among us face similar barriers and obstacles. If my transparency about my journey to discovering healing can help someone else, all the better.

Somewhere along the way, I learned to bury my hurt deep within myself, so much so that I built walls, wore masks, and hid the despair from others, even myself. I did not know that unresolved trauma remains in our bodies; it festers like cancer. My remedy was to fill the empty spaces pain had left behind with everything I could and discovered that only God could fill me.

Besides acknowledging God, what one should do when they feel pain inside again and again or cannot seem to heal, is not clear to me. One thing is certain— healing may not always look like what we expect. This is my side of the story.

# Chapter 1

## Speeding Rocket Kid

Childhood stories and memories are a part of life. Recollections from childhood can immediately call emotions like happiness, sadness, or even embarrassment to mind. My own emotions during childhood fluctuated up and down.

Emotionally, it felt like I was juggling balls. As one ball went up, I was happy for a minute, and then I was sad when that same ball came down. The ball went up. I was happy once again. But once the ball came down this time, I was angry. I could never feel any constant emotion for an extended period of time.

Life as a child felt unstable and unpredictable for the most part. Certain instances in my childhood were not mere moments but crucial to understanding who I am as a woman now. Combing through memories made me see how much of that little girl is still inside of me.

Throughout every stage of my life, I have always been different. Whenever others had the chance, they would remind me of my differences. Around the age of seven, I became more aware of these differences.

I was about a year and a half older and academically slower than the other kids in my classroom, and I started school later because of my late birthday. Technically, I was two grades behind. I also had to repeat first grade because I wasn't attending school enough the year before because of constant moving.

I used to avoid sharing my age with other children. Whenever my age was brought up, they would tease me. I remember something different from those moments— persistent, daily, and unrelenting teasing. Nowadays, it would be called bullying, but I thought being teased was a part of growing up. I just received more than my fair share.

The biggest telltale signs of my differences were the bumps, tumors, dark brown spots covering my entire body, and a condition that was hard to pronounce and understand. My mama and I shared similar physical traits, whereas my brother had a small trace of the brown spots on his body.

I despised being different because I was continually singled out. To make matters worse, my classmates feared me and my condition, so they avoided me. Whenever I would ask a kid from another class to play with me, there was always another kid interfering like a referee throwing down a penalty flag to stop play.

"You don't want to play with Radscheda; she has cooties," the interfering kid would say. They weren't talking about that fictitious childhood disease game.

My academic struggles also started in the first grade. I was unable to read. Back then, I believed that adults knew everything and could be trusted, but I soon found out otherwise. The school officials at my school had the best intentions but did not have it all together. They often misplaced me in "special classes" because of my genetic disorder, not my intelligence.

The teachers in those special classes considered me lazy and told me I would not be able to learn much due to the presumed limitations of my condition. In the past and even today, I have questioned myself: *Can I be smart and have a condition at the same time? Is my health the reason I'm not smart? What makes me so unlucky?* My heart made me feel like I could do anything— if only others allowed me to try.

Reading became harder, and I struggled even more when I moved to the next grade. In the second grade, I was assigned to a group of students with reading weaknesses who needed extra instruction. It was called "The Blazing Orange" reading group; however, it was not the lowest-level reading group.

Some others around me were unlucky too. I was not the only one longing for acceptance. My memory of a particular school incident is as fresh as if it were yesterday. Each Blazing Orange group member read a section from a *Scholastic News* magazine about leopards and their spots. It was finally time for the last reader of the day. James was his name; however, our class called him names because he stuttered.

James was a lot bigger than everyone in class; he was even bigger than the fourth graders in our school. Everyone in the class sat in pairs, but James sat alone at an over-sized desk near the teacher's assistant in the front of the classroom. He was badgered far more than I was, and I felt sorry for him.

The boys in the classroom would always mimic his stutter and call him "Porky Pig," while the girls laughed out loud and yelled, "Th-th-th-that's all, folks!" James would obnoxiously laugh out loud and join in the laughter. The way he let on, you would have thought the jokes weren't about him. Yet, in order to fit in, he would do anything.

In one instance, the class dared James to lick the cafeteria floor from the serving line to his assigned seat. They promised him friendship and to play with him on the playground, so James licked the floor while holding onto his small Incredible Hulk metal lunch box.

For a second, he had some instant friends once he got to the table. Shortly afterward, the boys decided not to play with James on the playground. Everyone has played the fool from time to time. There was no exception to the rule for James and me, and most likely just about everyone else.

My desire for friends was probably just as strong as James'. Personally, I was not going to embarrass myself just to have a few friends. Most of the time, I stayed under the radar in the classroom. I didn't want the jokes to backfire on me. So, I sat there and waited for my turn to be the butt of jokes. A part of me wanted to speak out on his behalf. On the other hand, I was incapable of standing up for myself, either.

In James' case, reading was like pulling teeth when the time came. No different than any other day, he began to stutter through the small six-sentence paragraph from the magazine. James kept pleading with the teacher throughout the lesson to stop reading. The other students and even our teacher must have become tired of him reading because they began to entertain themselves with other things.

They'd glance up with irritation on their faces, roll their eyes, tap their feet, and exhale loudly. When James needed a little push from being stuck on a word, our teacher would peek up and prompt him with the correct pronunciation. Some group members started reading other parts of the magazine, and one of them even fell asleep. Not me, though.

I followed along with James, giving him my undivided attention. As I saw it, I was like him, butchering words at times. I sometimes couldn't sound out a word or recognize it properly because my mind played tricks on me.

Even with several degrees under my belt, my mind still does this. I would quickly skip over words as if they did not exist back then. Even though I tried hard, I couldn't grasp vowel and consonant phonetic blends to read fluently.

I used to gather dandelions when I was a child. I would blow the seeds away and make wishes— wishing I looked like other kids and could learn things faster without even trying. I had an active imagination like most children.

It was nice to imagine myself reading as fast as my classmates in the advanced reading groups and having my teacher praise me for my remarkable reading abilities. I laugh out loud about it now, but I even believed eating Smarties candy would make me smarter and read better. It's funny what we believe and what we do as children.

No matter how much I wished, how many Smarties I ate, or how hard I tried, I could not read like the other kids. After becoming an adult, I learned most of my academic struggles were due to the learning disability of dyslexia along with speaking debilities called tongue-tie and cluttering disorder.

A tongue-tie occurs when a thick band of tissue binds the tongue's tip to the mouth's floor. It was something a simple surgical procedure could have corrected, whereas cluttering is a speech fluency and language disorder that would have to be worked on over time. As for the other conditions, they could not be fixed.

Just like other aspects of me, my way of speaking has always been different. The cluttering disorder interfered with my ability to communicate clearly. It is difficult to forget the constant advice I received from my parents, teachers, others, and people today— to slow down, speak louder, and think before speaking. Regardless of how much slower, louder, or how much I thought and planned before I spoke, people still had difficulty understanding me then and now.

As a result of the untreated tongue-tie, my speech was complicated and delayed, causing more difficulties over time. Additionally, a seizure disorder caused problems with reading comprehension, short-term memory, and writing. These unaddressed learning impediments directly contributed to my academic and social hardships at school. My emotional and physical health gradually declined with the progression of each disorder.

Back to the story of James, I suspect he wanted to divert the shame from himself and grab the attention of our teacher and the reading group. Suddenly, James paused reading the *Scholastic News* magazine article about the leopard. He stumbled over his words but managed to blurt out,

"You look like you've stolen some spots from a leopard."

Like how President Obama dramatically signified the end of a speech by kissing two fingers, dropping the microphone, and saying, "Obama out!"— nothing better could follow it. The five members of the Blazing Orange reading group and the other color-titled reading groups in the class began to snicker.

A deep sense of shame and embarrassment washed over me. I instantly put my head down on the reading table as if I was playing a game of "heads up, seven up" all by myself. The game may still be played in classrooms now with directions somewhat like this: All the students put their heads face down on their desks so they can't see anyone. Then, they put their thumbs up. Next, the student selected to be "it" stands in front of the class and, at the appointed time, goes around the classroom to pull the thumbs of individual students.

After the student who is "it" chooses whose thumbs to pull, the rest of the class raises their heads to guess who pressed their thumbs down. The only difference was that I had a rolled-up magazine in my hand where my thumb should have been, and I was playing the game alone.

"A leopard is walking around without spots!" one girl yelled. This added to the drama. I felt my stomach knot, and my heart was racing. Everyone in the class began chuckling again.

"Recess time!" shouted the teacher's assistant. The students jumped up from their seats and ran out of the classroom. Recess and gym time were my favorite parts of the day. My odds were different on the playground and in the gym.

Even though I was academically slower, I was always chosen first for gym activities. All the kids, including the boys, couldn't keep up with me in terms of speed and athletic ability. There was only one arena where my academic challenges, bumps, and spots didn't matter—when I was running.

Everyone wanted me to be their partner or teammate because I was an all-around athlete. In that one arena, my name changed from "Spotted Girl," "Bumpy," and "Dummy Girl" to the notorious "Cheetah Girl." I embraced that title proudly. I realize now that it didn't have as much of a positive connotation as I had thought. Cheetahs are known as the fastest land animals, but like me, they also have black spots all over their bodies.

Immediately following recess, our teacher informed us about a writing contest our school and the local newspaper were sponsoring. There were no restrictions on the topic of the writing contest. Our teacher asked us to brainstorm as everyone sat at their desks.

At the time, I felt defeated and went home without any ideas. When I arrived home, I told my mama about the writing contest and the lack of a topic for the contest. She suggested I place the contest flyer under my pillow that night.

Mama and I had this same ritual with my spelling words. We believed God would ensure that I retained the spelling words if I slept over them after studying. She believed that God could do anything, and that He would provide me with an idea for the writing contest. God delivered as usual. I skipped breakfast at school and went to my classroom to write the idea He had placed in my head overnight.

The story was about a girl who was teased for her learning disabilities and for having spots and bumps all over her body. The teased girl ran fast like a speeding rocket, so fast that people could not see her spots, bumps, or limitations. It also mentioned how she had a lot of friends because they could not see her spots and bumps.

Hesitantly, I wrote "The Speeding Rocket Kid" at the top of the paper, slowly walked to my teacher's desk, and handed it to her. She grimaced, her thin smile revealing the silver braces that looked like railroad tracks attached to her teeth.

I pulled out the books I had bought earlier that week at the book fair after I walked back to my desk. By happenstance, I glanced up to see tears streaming down my teacher's cheeks as she read my story. She hastily exited the classroom and handed my paper to the teacher's assistant.

Looking back on that incident, I presumed my teacher needed a moment to gather herself. When I turned toward the teacher's assistant, she winked and smiled. I smiled from within. Being much shorter than my classmates, my feet began to swing in the air as I sat at my desk.

A few weeks later, the school day began as usual with greetings of "Good Morning!" and "Will everyone rise for the Pledge of Allegiance?" Everyone stood and placed their right hand on their chest before reciting the pledge. James was stuttering as the class sat down, still trying to finish the pledge. All of a sudden, the principal's voice blared through the intercom system that she had a special announcement.

Completely demolishing the pronunciation of my name, the principal announced, "Congratulations to Radscheda Nobles on winning the writing contest!" She read my story over the intercom and asked me to come to the office to accept my prize. Everyone in the class began drumming on their desks out of excitement, and I could even hear some of my new fan club next door.

Overjoyed, my teachers also stood up and clapped. Our primary teacher instructed everyone to calm down and get ready for reading; I was then directed to get my hall pass. My teacher's smile gleamed as she handed me the pass, and I skipped down the halls with a wide Kool-Aid smile.

Once I returned to the class, everyone gathered around me and my first-place ribbon. It was an odd feeling but a good one as well. For the first time among my peers, I was surrounded by positive words and smiles of acceptance, not disgust.

The school and the local newspapers highlighted the "Speeding Rocket Kid" story, which became my first published work. I finally felt accepted and favored. I had earned the attention of my teachers and, most importantly, my peers. I thought there was actually a possibility that I could be smart *and* have a disability. I realized my smartness looked different, and I just needed others to chime in on it.

I could not wait to go back to school and float in my moment of stardom, even if I wasn't sure how long it would last. Over the weekend, we moved. The exciting moment occurred on a Friday, and I started a new school by the following Monday. It would seem like this would be a good thing for me, but it wasn't. Not at all.

And so it went again, another school year filled with tears and struggles. I began to wonder if writing another paper would earn me favor among my new teachers and classmates. People, no matter their age, have opinions and will always have them; however, other people's opinions bullied me. There was a constant sense of pressure and a need to be different from who I was. A child should never experience such feelings. No one should, not even an adult.

I detested being different and didn't want anything to do with it. If I could go back in time, I would challenge my teachers, "Don't judge a book by its cover." I would also add, "Judging a book by its cover could cause you to miss out on a great book." Many people we cross paths with will miss out on a good book or a good person.

I had finally found acceptance at my old school, only to have that ripped away and replaced with more teasing and isolation at my new school just because my genetic disorder made me different. This wasn't the last time my illness would rob me, causing me to experience ebbing highs and lows in my life. Life became quite fluid for me, never maintaining one constant state. Although I could not always ride the waves of life, at other times, I was able to do so. I probably would have braced myself if I knew what was heading my way around the corner.

Chapter 2

She Ain't My Mama

The game of dominoes isn't typically a popular game of choice, and I never really played it the way it was intended. I preferred lining up the oblong tiles, flicking the first domino, and watching them tumble into one after another. As a child, the sound of dominoes clinking as they struck each other fascinated me.

Life can follow the same pattern of the domino effect. One choice or situation can trigger an unstoppable chain of events. Life made an example out of me. Yet things are more complicated in life and don't line up as easily as dominoes.

My peers and teachers consistently reminded me of my limitations and medical condition throughout my school years; the taunting continued until it became normal to me. My disorders and disabilities weren't my fault; I couldn't take the blame. I certainly didn't sign up for them, but perhaps my mama did for both my brother and me.

In my mind, what I'd call "Draft Day" seems like it was yesterday —the day my mama and I had a conversation on the flower-patterned light brown couch with removable cushions from the Heilig-Meyers furniture store. I was around eight years old.

"Precious, you have inherited the family curse, Neurofibromatosis," Mama informed me.

Perhaps, she said, "disease." I heard "curse." It was as if I was shattered, confused, sad, angry, and hurt all at once. Tears began to flow down my cheeks, and I yelled,

"I have nothing like you. My appearance is nothing like yours!"

Mama's upper body was deformed and misshapen from NF-induced scoliosis; tumors large and small ran up the entire length of her body. The bitter truth was evident; I could see tumors on my arms, back, chest, and legs, but my mind told me otherwise. *She has a different condition than I do.*

From that moment, my feelings spiraled out of control. I disassociated myself and my identity from her and the disease she had. Like the little boy Harpo in *The Color Purple* shouted, "She ain't my mammy" to his step-mother, Celie (played by Whoopi Goldberg), my mama became "She ain't my mama" too.

Throughout my rebellious teenage years, my feelings about her and her disease came to a head. I was filled with mixed emotions, and at any point, I could explode. That woman and I were constantly in a tug of war about everything: clothes, boyfriends, friends, hoop earrings, cleaning my room, chores...the list goes on.

Like other girls my age, everything she said fell on deaf ears. I wanted a normal life, maybe even another life. When I reached junior high school, the family curse had an even greater impact on me.

Junior high school years are challenging for anyone, but they are especially tough for those who are not part of the in-crowd. As much as I tried to fit in, I could not. Like many girls, I struggled with self-image and self-worth. I never liked what I saw in the mirror. My peers inherited big butts and boobs from their mothers, but I inherited spots and tumors. So, there I was— surrounded by all these pretty girls— bumpy and unnoticed until people sought me out to tease or talk about me.

I kept my mama and how she looked a secret during my school days. Keeping the family medical history quiet made it possible for me to enjoy real friendships. Even my closest friends knew very little about our troubled relationship and the family disease. Only a few select friends would be invited over, and I would not permit my mama to attend school functions.

I remember an occasion in gym class when I tried to change into my gym clothes inside the restroom. My physical education teacher blocked my entrance to the restroom stall. Using a clipboard, she pointed toward the locker room.

"Radscheda, you need to dress out," she rasped in her hoarse voice. She directed me to the area where I was to get dressed, where I sat down on a bench.

I had school pictures to take that day, which was different from most days. Usually, I would wear my gym clothes under my regular school clothes to conceal my bumps and tumors and prevent me from being teased. That particular day, I had planned to change clothes in the bathroom stall in the locker room.

I refused to move from the bench with the attitude of Rosa Parks as the other girls ran out of the locker room already dressed in gym clothes. The PE teacher stood over me, her face directly in mine. The smell of her heavy breath reeking of smoke hit my face as she bit out, "You are going to lose points for not dressing up today. Please come out of the locker room now!"

"No, I have my gym clothes," I replied. "Can I change in the bathroom stall?"

After exchanging a couple of remarks, the teacher led me to her small office where I could see paint peeling off the walls. She turned to me as she picked up the phone receiver and asked for my home number and the name of a parent. Out of defiance, I boisterously recited my phone number and Mama's full name.

As she waited for someone to answer the phone, the PE teacher pleaded with me to change into my gym clothes. I had no need to worry. Surely, Mama would understand my dilemma. The PE teacher hurriedly explained the situation to my mama as soon as she answered. The teacher's face held that deer-in-the-headlights look as she signaled me to the phone. She handed me the receiver, and I placed it next to my ear with a smile as wide as J.J. Evan's from the *Good Times* television show.

My mama often resorted to her mama bear instincts during times like this. No matter what you did to her, she would tear you a new hole if you messed with my brother and me. I leaned my ear into the phone. "This issue will be discussed today with the principal," Mama assured me.

This meant she was coming to my school. *Oh, my goodness,* I exclaimed in dismay to myself. *Why didn't I just dress out or lose dress-out points?* I saw Mama leaving the principal's office as I was walking to lunch. She slowly approached me in the hallway. *Thank God, I am all alone*, I remember thinking.

"Precious, no one else is going to bother you about this issue anymore. You can dress out in the bathroom stall for gym class," Mama announced.

I looked up at the exit sign above her head as if she wasn't there. My eyes rapidly scanned the area back and forth for other students. I did not want to be seen with her. I was caught off guard when one of my friends approached us and asked if I was heading to lunch. I quickly distanced myself from Mama and walked away without saying a word. Not even an "I'll see you in the afternoon."

"Is that your mother?" A friend of mine asked.

"No," I said, "She ain't my mama."

When I glanced back at Mama, I was pretty sure she heard what I said. She lowered her head and walked out the door. It made me feel awful. Then again, I had told her to stay away from my school.

She started the whole thing. In elementary school, she would drop me off and leave even after I begged her to accompany me into the school. Now, she wanted to come to my junior high school. There was no way I was going to have that.

As I grew older, my opinions about my mama remained relatively unchanged. My attitude was still, "She ain't my mama." When I reflect on it, most of the time I spent with her, I was often accompanying her on errands. I watched her being singled out and teased for what seemed like a lifetime. A casual trip to the grocery store was never normal for us. The horrified, disgusted looks on people's faces were too much for me. So, I joined the bandwagon. I would stand from afar embarrassed, thinking, "She ain't my mama."

One particularly long shopping day, I wanted to crawl under a rock. Several young people were playing tag in the car next to us at a traffic light. One of them was a young man we had seen a few minutes before at a gas station. He pointed at my mama, appearing to have a conversation about her in the car.

I also remembered seeing the other people in the car at the gas station when I had gone into the store earlier to pay for the gas and buy a snack. Mama looked over at them and waved with a smile. She always seemed as if she was oblivious to her disease and the way other people viewed her.

One of the passengers from the car got out at the traffic light and knocked on our window. I slithered down the back seat. He was entertaining his audience in the car, but when he looked back at my mama, he saw a middle finger pressed hard against the glass.

She told him where to go. The light turned green, and she put her foot on the gas pedal and sped off.

Through the back window of the car, I smiled and giggled. Cars were swerving around the man still standing in the middle of the street. Mama had won that battle, but there was always more to come. I turned back around, catching her eyes in the rearview mirror. She was smiling too.

Our next destination, the grocery store, was an even more humiliating scene. The moment Mama walked into the store, it was as if people had seen a ghost. Patches of shoppers stopped in their tracks with their carts. Some even dropped food on the floor and gasped. One little boy pointed at my mama and called out to his mother, "Is she a monster?"

His mom hid him behind her overweight body. *Really fat woman*, I thought. "Fat woman" wasn't the actual word that came to mind though.

This kind of situation happened all the time; it was getting old. Mama walked around like a queen bee. She carried her head high, showed no shame, and did not let the negative attention affect her shopping. I was always one aisle or two away during any grocery trip with her. As we left to put the groceries in the trunk, people stared from inside the store and as they departed. My mama walked to the car's trunk and said, "I guess they didn't get enough of me."

She walked to the driver's side door, put on her pink sunglasses, tossed her Jheri curls, and drove away. While I was too embarrassed to reciprocate support in any of these situations, Mama always walked with her dimples, self-assurance, and pride in stride.

Recalling that specific shopping trip reminds me of my mama's uninvited visit to one of my track meets. The ability to run like a cheetah carried over to junior high school, where I was one of the fastest girls in the school. I was preparing to run the 200-meter dash when I saw Mama hiding under the deserted bleachers. The starting pistol went off. I crossed the finish line first, then glanced in her direction as I celebrated. She was walking away with her arms raised in the air. We never discussed her visit to the track meet. I'm not even sure if she attended any other events.

A few months later, Mama was admitted to the hospital. My boyfriend and I visited her before seeing *Crooklyn* at the dollar theater. She was shocked when I walked through the hospital room door. We watched several episodes of *Matlock* for about an hour on the television attached to the hospital wall.

After telling her we had to leave, Mama asked me if I could stay a little longer. This time with her felt different; my heart wouldn't let me say no. I smiled and said yes. My boyfriend and I decided to go to the next movie showing. As I stood beside her, I could not stand seeing her lying in the hospital bed, knowing how strong I knew she was.

My dad and Mama had been arguing again. This time, he didn't visit her in the hospital. I'm not sure what made this situation different from the others. I could only imagine what she was thinking and feeling. My love for my mama was strong, but I couldn't accept all that came with her. It felt like NF took everything away from our family.

After spending another hour with her, I hugged Mama and headed out of the room to go to the movies. As I was shutting the door, she called out, "Precious!"

I peeked my head back in the door.

"Promise me that you will take care of your brother and yourself!" she said.

"Mama, everything is going to be fine," I replied, "I will call you in the morning."

I kept thinking of her while watching the movie. It was a brutal film to watch with the mother dying and the family grieving. I recall crying so hard that I lost interest in continuing to watch it. The ride home was long. Once I arrived home, I told my boyfriend to call me the next day. I could not get my mama off my mind.

The following day, I called her and told her that my brother and I were heading to school. Other than being Valentine's Day, nothing seemed out of the ordinary. I could not wait to get to school and receive Valentine's cards from other possible admirers and friends.

On the way to my English class, I admired the teddy bear and Valentine's card I received. I put them away and began working on the assignment written on the board. Once I finished, I put my head on my desk while waiting for my classmates to finish their tasks. The phone in the classroom rang.

I felt a soft tap on my shoulder. Startled, I jerked my head up. I thought my teacher was trying to direct me back to my assignment and rushed to explain that I had already completed my tasks. However, she interrupted me and asked one of my classmates to accompany me to the office.

We headed to the office, and I saw the guidance counselor waiting at the entrance. The counselor gestured for me forward when I reached the corner of the hall. She placed her hand on my back and guided me into her office, where my dad, a neighbor, and my brother were seated. That is when I heard words that changed my life forever—my mama was dead.

It was hard to breathe, understand, and think. My heart pounded. *She was only thirty-six years old, she was only thirty-six years old, she was only thirty-six years old*, I kept repeating in my mind. I should have told her that she *was* my mama and loved her. I felt guilty. Like falling dominoes, this one defining moment set off a series of events in my life.

# Chapter 3

It's surreal to have your entire life fall apart all at once. Everything important I possessed was taken from me all in one day: the essence of love, my mama, a sense of myself, and what made my family.

It's easy to smile when things in life are going well. But when things go south, it can be a devastating experience. At that moment, it felt like everything in my life was coming to a breaking point. What does a girl do when everything under her feet is crumbling, spiraling out of control with nothing to hold onto?

I don't remember much of what happened immediately after I received the bad news. It's strange because I have an excellent memory. From the age of four onwards, I can recall many memories clearly. Yet on this particular day, I cannot remember how my brother and I got home from school, whether my dad hugged me, if I ate dinner that night, or how I got into bed.

The next day, however, all the details are vivid. It was February 15. My body felt sore all over as if I had just returned from track practice. I struggled to open my eyes; crying all night had caused tears to crystallize on my eyelids. I sat up on the bed and untangled myself from my purple sheets. Propping my back against the wall, I attempted to remove what crust I could. The crust would not leave my eyes, no matter how hard I tried.

I headed blindly down the narrow hallway to the bathroom. My eyes burned as soon as I flicked on the light switch. My reflection in the mirror resembled a basset hound dog, the bags so large they caused my eyes to droop. The whites of my eyes were fire red like I had spent the night drinking. My cheeks, mouth, nose, and earlobes were streaked with my dried tears. *What a hot mess*!

I braced my small framed body and elbows on the bathroom countertop. Then, I slightly turned the clear knob on the faucet to get hot water. I held a balled-up pink washcloth under the stream of water. I rubbed my face vigorously to relieve the pain. It wasn't literal, but I was trying. I threw the washcloth down without brushing my teeth and hurried to the kitchen to phone my mama.

My hand trembled as I punched the hospital's telephone number into the phone. Phone calls were our morning routine when Mama was in the hospital. As soon as my brother and I woke up for the day, I would call her to let her know we were on the way to school. We followed the same routine when my brother and I returned home. While holding the receiver close to my right ear, I thought to myself that maybe it was all a dream. I have always dreamed about death since I was a child and still do.

At the moment, I desperately needed this to be one of those dreams. A stranger answered after several rings. Like the pause button on my remote control, I froze. *This isn't Mama's soft voice*, I thought before responding, *or her "Good morning, Precious."*

I wondered briefly if this person could take a message for my mama. With two fingers, I abruptly hung up on the unfamiliar voice. An avalanche of thoughts and feelings bombarded me at once. *It wasn't a dream.* It was a real-life nightmare. Her hospital bed had already been assigned to another patient.

The ugly truth became apparent. I had to face the cruel reality that my mama would not return home. Tears poured from my puffy eyes again. I collapsed in agony to the floor and sobbed uncontrollably, crying out to God for mercy. I cried, and I cried, soaking my shirt with all my tears.

Once I regained control, I went straight to my parents' closet, opened it, and stood there for a while. Their clothes were tightly packed in the closet; each had their own side. Mama's clothes were mainly on the right side of the closet. With my forearm, I separated her clothes to one side. She had windbreaker suits in every color and pattern you could imagine. I could see her smiling from dimple to dimple as I went through the clothes.

Her Sunday best outfit, a green skirt suit with black stripes and a black scarf, caught my eye. It was a suit she loved and took several pictures in. I removed it from the closet and held it close to my aching body, smelling the faint scent of her red and black perfume. The name of the perfume escapes me, but I frequently still see it in Family Dollar stores.

It was strange to smell her scent since she hadn't been home in weeks. Perhaps my mind was playing tricks on me again. After fumbling around a bit, I glanced down at the closet floor and saw her double-knotted tennis shoes. Her shoes remained in a double knot so that she could slip them on; one of her hands was unusable.

I became weary after looking through the clothes. As I left the room, my attention was drawn to Mama's dresser. I found a black banana clip and her clip-on earrings on top of it. In the strangest of all circumstances, I truly can't remember whether she had her ears pierced or not. Mama kept clip-on earrings as a means to keep her independence; she could put them on without having anyone in the family assist her.

Tears coursed down my face as I picked up the black banana hair clip. I could see myself brushing and putting the clip in her Jheri curls. I used to huff and puff like the wolf in the three-little pigs' story when she asked me to put it in her hair. The only time my mama asked me to do anything for her was to put the clip in her hair. If I were given one more chance with her, I would do anything she asked without hesitation.

Nothing could have prepared me for the feelings, the mind-numbing pain that took residence in my entire body, especially inside my heart. Mama's death was completely unexpected. Her last stay at the hospital was like any other revolving hospital door encounter, and the doctor was planning her return home. Mama and I had spoken earlier that morning and planned her return home as well.

I tried to piece together what had happened to Mama between the time I had spoken to her and the time I received the news that she had died. It's difficult for anyone to lose a loved one, but something about the scenario surrounding my mama's death never sat well with me. As a minor, I was prevented from investigating or questioning her doctors. I didn't have the maturity to think of asking my dad what happened.

It's too late now. Not fully knowing the details of the mysterious circumstances surrounding her death has haunted me throughout my life. It seems I'll have to wait for my Maker to seek revenge and justice on her behalf.

My dad was washing clothes at a laundromat near the house when he spoke to my brother and me about the living arrangements we would have after the funeral. He asked if we would like to stay in our current home or move back to Virginia, where his family was and where we had lived before. Both of us agreed we wanted to stay in the house; some part of us didn't want to move.

I was conflicted emotionally, but I accepted our decision and pretended there was nothing wrong. Our living situation had always been uncomfortable for me. Once, I remember during an argument between my parents, my mama told me I could not go with my dad because he was not my biological father. My dad was actually only the biological father of my brother. Because he's the only father I've ever known, I've always called him dad; but when he caused harm, he was my stepdad.

I began to ask myself, *What am I going to do now? Who is going to take care of me? And who is going to raise me now? Where are the blueprints and plans?* Mama hadn't left any instructions for me. I found out later, as an adult, that she attempted to make plans for me to stay with different family members before she passed away. As a result, I often wonder if my mama would have wanted me to stay with my stepdad.

A loved one's loss is indescribable. Whenever I felt like crying, I would put on a fake smile. Surely the pain I was experiencing was similar to the pain my mama experienced giving birth to me, and perhaps now I was experiencing some type of labor pain after she passed away.

It wasn't fair that Mama died. Her loss was too much for me to bear. I still had a lot to learn, and I needed her. As a child, I dreamed of being the daughter of a different mother. Just for a moment, I needed a plea bargain or maybe even a genie. In exchange for my mama's return, I would have sacrificed some of my time on earth.

Perhaps I was being a bit selfish here, considering how much Mama suffered throughout her entire life. Her suffering included a chronic disease, being denied unconditional love from those who mattered, mistreatment from others and me, and experiencing domestic violence. Mama never experienced true peace until she passed away.

My life was unraveling.

Family members, friends, and neighbors called and visited my family at our house to comfort us. I kept hearing variations of the polite phrase, "Sorry for your loss." As if I had lost a dog or something. I found that to be so tiresome in and of itself. Numbness set in, and nothing made any sense in my world.

Several days later, we traveled to Mama's hometown to bury her. Arrangements were made for the funeral at the church my family attended before our last move. Dad, my brother, and I went to the wake before Mama's funeral. It wasn't held at a church, but I can't recall the exact location.

I managed to look normal at the wake, but I didn't feel normal. Those around me once again told me how sorry they were and how my mama had passed on to a better place. One of her friends asked me, "How do you feel, sweetheart?"

I know there's a saying that you're not supposed to answer a question with another question; however, before I knew it, I blurted out, "How in the hell do you think I should feel? The woman that brought me into the world is gone!"

The woman must have been caught off guard because her eyes got as big as quarters, and she quickly walked away. I was wrong. My parents had not raised me to be disrespectful to adults. I genuinely needed a pass from home training that day.

The first time I saw Mama in her casket was at the wake before the funeral. I touched her cold face and told myself she wasn't my mama. I quickly moved away from the imposter lying in the casket. My mama was a warm, friendly, and sincere person. That woman in the coffin resembled none of those qualities.

During the funeral service to honor Mama, I tried to keep my emotions at bay. I suddenly started crying uncontrollably. I could no longer hear any part of the service; it was as if I was underwater. It took a few moments for the clogging in my ears to let up, but I could hear the muffled voice of the preacher instruct the ushers to open the casket lid.

I stared at the casket. Mama had on makeup, which she didn't normally wear. I shed even more tears. Then I lost it so badly that my auntie, Mama's baby sister, escorted me away from the casket during the service. Riding to the cemetery was somewhat of a blur.

My mama wasn't the only one to be buried that day. I also lost myself. As they were throwing dirt over her casket, it felt like they were burying me. I was suffocating; I couldn't breathe. I tried to take long, deep breaths. There didn't seem to be a way out of what felt like a smothering grave, no way out at all. While I wasn't literally being buried with Mama, I was at her graveside struggling to free myself from the heavy, oppressive pain.

We walked to our Subaru after the burial. As I waited for my dad to open the car doors, I glanced at the passenger door. My mama should have been standing there, but no one was there. I knew right then that my life would be forever changed; it would never be the same.

I was the most like her out of all the people I knew. We shared similar personality traits. Her absence made my life feel alienated from everyone else, even though I had a brother and dad. It might have been the guilt I felt for not always treating her well. It was true, you really don't know what you have until it's gone.

Another adage that says, "time heals all wounds," I didn't find to be true. I wonder if there is a right or wrong way to grieve. Or is there a limited set time for the process? The pain from the loss of my mama was like a shadow that followed me everywhere I went, but it was like a boulder too. It was heavy to carry. I couldn't accept that I would never see her again, at least not on earth.

I'm not sure how long the grieving process took for my dad and brother. My brother never talked about her death. And my dad moved on to other companions before even removing my mama's belongings, which added to my hurt. I believe no one is ever ready to accept someone who might attempt to replace their mother. Even to this day, the house remains exactly as Mama left it, minus a few things from the other woman.

I closed myself off from my feelings, the world, and everyone around me like a turtle retreating into a shell. I was utterly lost and afraid. I slept on life, refusing to move. I learned very quickly during the days, weeks, months, and years ahead that there is nobody who loves a daughter as much as her mother. Before I knew who I was, my mama knew. It may sound crazy, but I thought accepting the healing process or moving on would cause me to forget about her. I hadn't been a very loyal daughter to my mama, but it's something I won't let happen again.

Some people grieve by staying busy, becoming a workaholic, or having a healthy social life. To put it bluntly, I stopped giving a f---k about life and anyone in it. Unfortunately, I stayed in my shell and refused to move on. Every time misfortune knocked on my door, I answered.

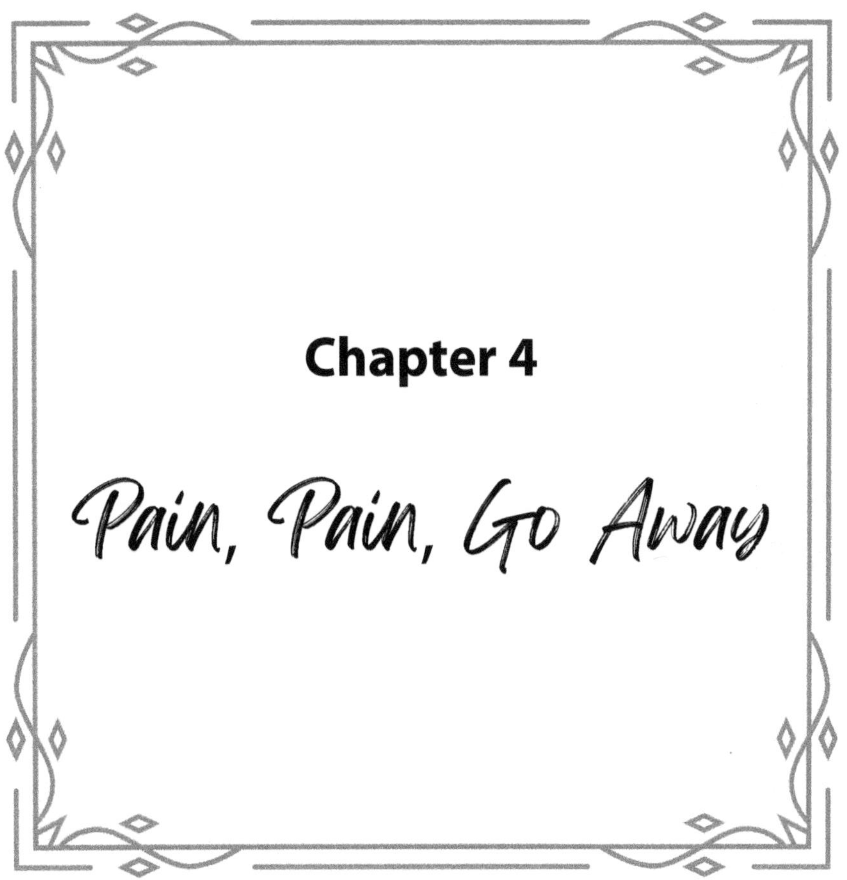

# Chapter 4

# Pain, Pain, Go Away

f I could, I would rewrite the nursery rhyme, "Rain, Rain, Go Away," as "Pain, Pain, Go Away, Never Come Again Another Day." Everyone goes through hardships and emotional bumps throughout life. Knowing that, however, doesn't make it any easier. The feeling of hurt is deeply personal, even if we all suffer from it. What should one do if the pain doesn't go away? I'm afraid I don't have an answer.

For as long as I can remember, the presence of pain never seemed to skip a beat in my life; it appeared in different phases. Like a receding tide, the anguish would lessen over time, then return occasionally. Sometimes the ache of it swallows me whole, transporting me back to the place where I once lived. Although my mama's death was my greatest sorrow, a subsequent occurrence at my new junior high shortly after her death was a close second.

Before losing my mama, my family moved from place to place, from one home to another. It got to a point where I lost track of the moves and new homes. I obtained my school records to determine how many schools I attended: a total of nine elementary schools, two junior high schools, and one high school. We often moved in the middle of the school year without notice. Because I moved around a lot, I had to say goodbye to friends abruptly, which was difficult for me as an introvert.

One move during the summer made it easier for me to build relationships with neighborhood boys. While I was growing up, I lived in neighborhoods composed mainly of boys and younger girls. The boys accepted me as one of them, even though I was better than them. Supposedly, a boy pulls a girl's ponytail when he likes her. When I liked a boy, I would run faster, mow him down, or throw a football better than he could.

My life as a teenager was effortless: blue jeans, T-shirts, sneakers, hoodies, and braids. I was also deodorant-free, which revealed my secret "mustiness." Only a few boys found my tomboyishness and mustiness appealing enough to make me their girlfriend. I usually made friends in elementary school by giving friendship necklaces and candy. As I grew older, I gave away another type of candy.

After Mama died, I started school back up as an eighth grader at a new junior high school. I usually felt alone, overlooked, and invisible around boys. Although I still hung out with the boys, our relationships began to change. Our conversations used to be about WWF wrestling and wrestlers like Hulk Hogan, Ric Flair, and The Great Kabuki. Now, they were about the hottest girls in school.

It felt more comfortable to hang out with boys since they were chill and nonjudgmental. I could be myself. I often wondered how I could stop being one of the boys and become someone they could love. Getting along with girls was a different story. I found them difficult. My name was always the subject of "he said, she said" stuff.

My tomboyishness and disease also made me feel uncomfortable in a crowd of girls. I felt uglier and feared I would have earned another nickname from my peers. Both Mama's death and my last year at junior high school were challenging and heart-wrenching for me. I needed something to fill the void left by my mama. Occasionally, a person or situation would temporarily fill the void, or at least I thought it did.

A boy from the "A-list" autographed my yearbook with the message, "I wish things could be different between us. I like you but don't want to ruin my reputation." I felt satisfied for a moment. Then I felt beaten down and rejected. I was always rejected by everyone— boys, girls, my family, teachers, and even strangers.

I longed to be accepted and to be part of a group. Yet, I was never truly part of anything— until this one time. During one teacher's workday, several boys and girls from the popular group at school met up at a friend's house to explore our sexual curiosity. The host of the gathering, a girl I had become close with, invited me.

One of the boys I liked was also invited. He had curls on the top of his head and faded sides. There was a connection between us. The heart-shaped drawings and bubble letters he drew that included his name and my name hinted at his affection.

Going to this unsupervised meet-up was exciting. A few girls and I were standing across the room when "Forever My Lady" by Jodeci started playing. My eyes were drawn to him as he talked to three other boys on a black leather couch.

I left the girl talk and headed in his direction. Everyone was watching us as we locked eyes. His attention never left me when he got up from the couch. He reached for my hand just as I stood in front of him. This was our jam.

Sometimes he would sing love songs on the phone to me in this Kermit the Frog voice affected by puberty. I didn't care what he sounded like. He liked ME—Radscheda Nobles! And he had absolutely no problem spreading the news.

Others, especially girls, would respond to our relationship by asking him, "Why do you like that ugly girl?" They would also be in my ear, "You are out of his league." or "He just wants easy sex from you." In my mind, I would be like, "B----! You are the one that let the boys have it their way like Burger King."

As far as I could tell, he genuinely cared about me, which had nothing to do with sex. We never had sex, even when I aggressively tried to throw the "P" on him. He would respond respectfully by saying, "Radscheda, you are unique" and "Just be you." In my head, everything centered around us, and we could talk and laugh about anything all night long.

While standing together in that moment with "Forever My Lady" playing in the background, the music paused. At least, I thought it did. Suddenly, a ripping sound could be heard across the room, and my shirt fell to the floor. Without turning around, I recognized the traitor's voice, the friend who had invited me.

"You are ugly and a bumpy mess," she said, "Why would you think anyone would want to be your friend, freak?"

I stood there speechless. My mind went blank. Goosebumps rose on my skin as a cool breeze hit my breast and back, adding to my existing bump of tumors. A faint sound of music could still be heard in the background, but I couldn't make out the lyrics.

Dazed, I continued to stand there shirtless in my confusion. At this point, my mind flooded with thoughts. *My secret is out*, I thought to myself. Apparently, my boyfriend was just as shocked, his actions slow as he drew me to his chest in order to shield my face. He covered my back with his arms as best as he could. Although he tried to conceal the tumors dotting my back, he was unable to do so.

He removed his shirt and placed the white oversized, sweaty Wu-Tang tee over my head. Anger bubbled inside me like a kettle. My eyes were filled with tears, and I still couldn't speak from embarrassment.

To this day, I am not sure what the mean girl expected to happen. Nobody laughed as I expected; the room became silent. The others gathered their belongings quietly and glanced at me with compassion and hurt in their eyes. She had failed in her attempt to shame me.

The next day, I just knew the story would spread like a virus throughout the school and be the gossip story of the day. No one ever spoke about it to my surprise; at least I never heard anything about it. I never told anyone about the experience until adulthood, but to this day the humiliation I felt is as fresh in my mind as the day it happened.

I broke up with that boyishly cute boy. I couldn't get over the embarrassment, even though he tried to prove his feelings hadn't changed. While passing each other in the hallway, anyone could sense our feelings for each other were still strong. I later found out that the traitor, aka a mean girl, liked him too. In hindsight, I gave her the fuel she needed to burn me. I promised myself that no one would ever be able to hurt me again or that I would ever feel out of control in a situation.

I wish someone would have told me that grief's sense of time does not operate like regular time. Grief held this tight grip on me. I didn't believe that happiness was even an option for me, so I made space for my pain. Like an occupant in a room of a house, my hurt still occupies a space inside me.

My mama's death, being shamed in front of my peers, other happenings in my life, and my sentiments about the disease forged strongholds in my life. Insecurity, pain, and a sense of fear ruled my life. They became my best friends for a long time. Together, they were like one bossy friend who tries to oversee everything. I found it difficult to separate myself from them.

The feelings became overwhelming, and I was unable to keep a proper perspective. One by one, my choices in life crashed into each other. I stopped running track, dropped out of high school, was homeless for several years, became a side chick, a cutter, and burned some bridges along the way. This was the point when I became a victim of my own choices, and brokenness set in.

# Chapter 5

## Tenderoni Girl

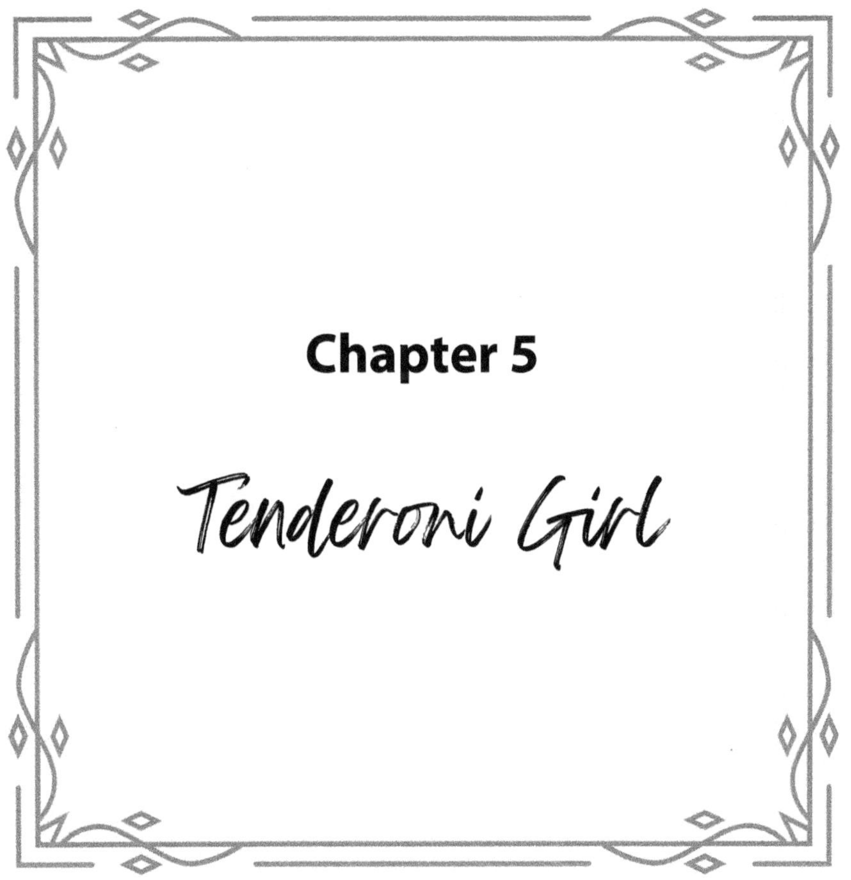

roken homes, relationships, and dreams are far too familiar to many people. Of course, not everyone experiences brokenness, but there are also many ways in which it can be interpreted. To me, it means the loss or the crushing of one›s self-will.

Brokenness came into the world long before I was born. I believe it's more than likely that everyone will experience it at some point in life without being given much of a choice— it happens to us somehow. Some of us have been broken more than others, like me.

Throughout my life, I have been defined by my shortcomings. When I look at my life, I can clearly see all the ways I fall short, trusting my own understanding instead of God's. The brokenness became more than part of my journey; it became my anchor. The crippling despair inside me was unresolved and persisted, resulting from unavoidable circumstances and my own sinful choices. Sometimes we become comfortable with dejection as I did, so much so that we adopt it as part of our identity.

My first sign of brokenness as a child was a fixation on the need for food to stay together. For example, I would not eat a sandwich if it fell apart. My feelings about broken crayons were the same. Ironically, now as an adult, I like it when my food falls apart. However, I thought togetherness meant perfect and better when I was a child.

After my mama passed away, I felt the family had fallen apart. I was done with my family, just like the crayons and sandwich. I left the family home after a few years. So many things were happening, many of them too hurtful to mention.

When I left, I took a few clothes and the 16 x 20 picture we had of Mama on the fireplace mantle. There was no way she would be disrespected or shoved into a closet to make room for the other woman. I found myself not only motherless but also unexpectedly homeless.

For about four years, I hopped from couch to couch, park bench to park bench, and shelter to shelter. My life was chaotic during that time, and I tried to get by any way I could. A life of survival was stressful and traumatic; it had its own consequences.

My fortune seemed to take another turn, at least I thought so. Just like in the story of *The Ugly Duckling*, my ugliness was only for a season. I transformed into a different kind of woman. As I grew older, men began to notice me.

I became known as "The Around the Way Girl." I was twenty-something years old, living in an urban area, independent, educating myself, no kids, chill, and had an hourglass body and a big butt. I still had those tumors, but they didn't stop me or the show.

Men found me attractive, but my relationships with them only summed up to friends with benefits. In those relationships, we would kick it and have sex whenever he could escape his obligations. To the street boys and the older men, I was the side piece, the side chick, and perhaps even the homewrecker.

I granted anything these men desired like the genie in *I Dream of Jeannie*. My main goal as a side piece was to rock it like I had the mic. I wanted to give them an experience to remember so good that when it came to the disease, they would not think about it or remember it. They would be like,

"What disease?" or "What tumors and spots?" Perhaps, the p——y was that good.

Regardless of who I was with in a relationship, we never talked about the tumors or spots on my body. It was as if NF didn't exist. Everything went on as usual; I never knew how they felt about them or if they just saw me as a woman or just a piece of "a——." I was okay with not talking about my disease, the elephant in the room.

I brushed off any conversations about my disease because they were awkward, embarrassing, and intimidating to some degree. As a young woman, I was not well educated on the ramifications of my illness and lacked a good understanding of my health condition. My willful ignorance was my way of not accepting myself. Refusing to accept and acknowledge reality as it is won't suffice in the long run.

To be clear, I was very selective about the men I chose —most of the relationships I had carried on for a while. It would be tempting to judge my choices, but I am not the only human being in the world who manipulated the opposite sex with their sexuality. The tattoo "freaky"

I got on my left arm left no doubt about the confidence I felt in my sexuality. It's doubtful that many men would reject freakiness.

Ironically, I am now embarrassed by the tattoo. Years ago, I was standing in line at Chick-fil-A and saw an older man with reddened skin holding onto a walker. In his elderly voice he quavered, "Are you still freaky, baby?" The top denture flew out of his mouth when he lewdly wiggled his tongue at me.

Sick to my stomach, I threw up a little in my mouth. I felt embarrassed because I would have enjoyed and accepted his question as a compliment at one point in my life and would have even reacted positively. I was good on the grandpa, though.

My people-pleasing behaviors were directed toward women as well. I sought not only their opinions but also their approval. In my mid-twenties, a few of my friends and I went to this club on the block. We searched for seats as we entered the club. I had seen several single tables, but one of the ladies yelled over the music that we needed two. I was a little puzzled because there were only a few of us. I pointed out two tables where we all quickly hustled because the club was beginning to fill up.

When we approached the tables, I was ushered to one table alone as the other ladies sat at another—this was by the request of my friends. They were truly not friends—I learned right then that they were ashamed of me. A part of me wanted to leave; however, I felt and looked fine as wine that night, so I stayed.

Those ladies, my so-called friends, underestimated me and the spell I had on the menfolk. Before the end of the night, I had an entourage full of men, and those ladies eventually joined my table. While I did not get a seat with them, I didn't need one after all. I danced the night away while the ladies I came with were relegated to chair dancing that night.

So much had not changed from the little girl in the "Speeding Rocket Kid" story to the "Tenderoni" girl. Crazy as it may sound, as a young woman, I tried to avoid rejection and gain acceptance by giving men great sex and being as sexually accommodating as they wanted me to be.

My worth and value had become wrapped around how others felt about me, so much so that I found myself constantly trying to prove my worth. It finally came to the point that I began to fulfill requests and desires even if those men showed me lacking character. Truthfully, I didn't want those kinds of relationships for myself. My morals told me those types of relationships were wrong and unhealthy.

However, I had a sense of control over them, something I lacked as a child. I knew I possessed the toy they wanted to play with, so I used this knowledge to control the situation. When I didn't want to be bothered, I wouldn't answer the phone or would pretend they didn't exist. I would also end the relationships without hesitation and with no explanation.

There was still a part of me that longed for and wanted more, but I often settled for a relationship with no strings attached. I didn't know if I could ever ask for more with my genetic disorder and all that came with it or if I should just be satisfied with what I received—I felt I could not ask for more.

My thought process towards sex and relationships was complicated. I was receiving some attention. Even though it was dangerous and unhealthy, situationships made me feel good and temporarily filled a void. In those moments, I felt wanted and received undivided attention, like I was someone special. This fueled my need for love, approval, and acceptance.

Busta Rhymes said it best, "On the flip side, these relationships left me feeling even more empty and alone." These relationships failed to include words like "I love you." Of course not, I was the side piece.

Even though I received attention, I had low self-esteem. The desire for attention was essential, and it still is. It didn't matter whether the behavior was positive or negative. I craved other people's attention regardless of the cost.

Strangely, as a side piece, I committed myself to one man at a time and remained loyal to him. Even today, I'm unsure of how to begin to explain it. Perhaps there has always been a good heart inside of me, or maybe I was still just a "tenderoni," a young woman looking for love and acceptance in the wrong places. Whatever the case, I wanted people to see me rather than my condition. And I was ready to be freed.

Rather than be trapped by my disease and pain, I need to move forward. My problem is that I don't know what to do. It's still easy for me to keep returning to my old behavior patterns simply because they're familiar.

# Chapter 6

# Merry-Go-Round

**P**laygrounds are one of the most enjoyable hallmarks of childhood. Children often hurtle towards the swings, slide, seesaw, sandbox, merry-go-round, or whatever else they love the most. My favorite was the merry-go-round, not the hot slide. Due to my rocket running skills, I was the permanent pusher on the playground. Reflecting on this childhood moment reminds me that life can sometimes seem like a merry-go-round.

Occasionally, other kids pushed me on the merry-go-round. Some kids remained on the merry-go-round until it stopped because they were scared. Not me; I'd like to jump off the merry-go-round while it was still rotating. I had no fear of letting go or where I would land. If only I had the same spirit as a child at this age.

I had a habit of taking the path of least resistance, doing only what I had to do. And I was having a hard time letting things go— the past, pain, people, mistakes, anger, clothes, birthday cards, and the list goes on and on. Of course, most people don't want to let go of things they like, but I don't understand why we often hold tightest to the things that hurt us.

I held onto the pain of Mama's death tightly with my whole being like a football player gripping a football as he makes a touchdown catch. I felt anchored to the pain; maybe it was guilt. My heart never fully healed, and I wore a cloak of shame. As my heart and mind continued to replay the lifetime of moments I had with her, I reflected on what I should have said and done. For example, I never said, "I'm sorry, you're my mama, and I love you." Never in a million years did I think I'd be doing life alone without my mama. Contrary to what I showed her, I have always needed her. When I was a child and couldn't handle things myself, she handled them for me.

Moving on was vital, but I was afraid I would forget her. And if I did accept her death, she would be gone forever. I didn't want to betray her like my dad did. He was back on the market immediately after Mama's death. He had new women within six months or less. Everyone's healing process is different of course; I get it. I was not ready to see him with other women or see him apart from Mama.

I wondered if he ever loved her and, if so, how he could be with these other women so soon. On top of that, he treated them better than Mama. That really hurt. I can't say much to that; I wasn't good to her either. It would have been helpful if my dad had allowed us a little more time to mourn and adjust. While most of his women were friendly, one was not so much. But that's another story for another day.

The fact was I really didn't want to do life without my mama. I have never been certain if it's possible for me to be happy without her or if I deserve to have the freedom she never knew. Unfortunately, she encountered a lot of abuse from many people, even from me. Regardless of what Mama received from others, she loved everyone unconditionally. She would also want me to be happy. Nothing compares to the love of a mother for her child.

In my heart though, I was waiting for my mama to return. The unfortunate truth was that she would never return to us, at least not on earth. It became clear that I would have to learn how to live without her and share her experiences as a teaching tool for myself as well as others. However difficult it may be to admit, I have physically made strides in life, but I am emotionally stunted. I am still troubled and deeply wounded.

I have been intensely sensitive to the emotions of others since a very young age, so much so that I absorb other people's feelings. I can feel not only their mental anguish but also their physical pain. As I sat with her in the hospital room the night before she passed away, I sensed Mama wanted to apologize for her part in our toxic relationship and some deeply scarring situations she placed me in due to her weaknesses. She desired to be free and forgiven, and there was so much unresolved between us. Perhaps I could have freed her soul if I had stayed to talk with her.

Although I didn't want her to suffer, a part of me did. It was only later that I realized the peace I failed to give my mama would severely hold me back in my search for an identity apart from my trauma. I was selfish like most teenagers at the time. I didn't understand about showing grace, God's love, or even forgiveness. It wasn't until much further in my journey that I discovered how God could change my life. Now I know better because my life has been transformed by life experiences and the love of God.

For many years, I ran in countless circles like the merry-go-round in my childhood. Finding myself at the same place in my life became all too familiar for me. My response to spinning in circles was always the same—I was ready to let go of my merry-go-round nightmare. After finally taking that leap, I soon found myself in another predicament. Surely, I'm not the only person who has ever found themselves in a place with no way out.

Often, we hear a lot about forgiving others, but we do not talk enough about how to forgive ourselves or the consequences of not forgiving ourselves. The truth is, I've never entirely been able to forgive anyone, not even myself. My regret is not forgiving Mama and not giving her the peace she desired. Withholding that peace came with a price.

Two of my biggest "aha" moments were: realizing that I had no idea who I was apart from my trauma and health condition because I had built my whole identity around both trauma and disease. And how not forgiving oneself made it difficult to honor and even see growth and healing.

# Part II

**"Some accessories we choose to wear and some we don't."**

*Whether it be just the right belt, cufflinks, purse, sunglasses, scarf, jewelry, or footwear—accessorizing clothing is a form of self-expression and fashion. Some accessories, however, cannot be removed and must accompany every outfit and occasion in life. On a journey of survival and self-acceptance, a woman attempts to detangle her mother's story from her own. Her mother's trauma, illness, and pain became permanent accessories that enhanced her ability to love others generously despite a life of suffering. The woman's greatest challenge in her quest for healing is to learn how to outfit herself with the accessories she inherited from her mother.*

**Dr. Radscheda R. Nobles**

# Chapter 7
## Our Belongings

It is difficult for me to define who I am apart from my trauma and disease. Trauma lies deep inside a person; one might even say it settles into their bones. It isn't just confined to the head, either. Trauma can be worn on the body, leaving a visible imprint that can be seen in eyes, facial demeanor, and even in the way a person carries themselves.

I believe trauma was stuck in my body. Even before learning about the genetic disease, I was already familiar with the trauma it can cause. People inherit more than just their parents' skin tone and eye color; we can also inherit their narrative and trauma. Like any parent, my mama entered parenthood with her own wounds and brokenness. I believe she wanted a better life for us, but she didn't anticipate how her childhood trauma would affect both her children and her husband.

Mama's name was Mamie Ann Nobles-Valentine. She was born to Harriett Nobles and Willie McCotter in 1958. Mama got the disorder of neurofibromatosis from her mama's side of the family, which had been in the family for approximately four generations. Mama became pregnant with me a year after

graduating from high school, hiding her pregnancy from others. Her grandmother on her father's side was the one who raised her.

When Mama's grandmother died unexpectedly, she was passed down to her aunt. Mama often told me that the only person she ever felt loved and wanted by was her grandmother. Other family members tolerated her only because of the disability check that came with her. From what I understand, she never lived with any of her parents. Without her parents around, I can only imagine how she felt.

I have no idea who my biological father is, and neither do any of my family members. Mama took that secret to the grave with her. Shortly after I was born, our living situation in Virginia with my great aunt was a short stay. We were kicked out of the house following a dispute Mama had with my auntie when I was about two years old.

My mama met my dad on my aunt's front steps just before we were thrown out. Their relationship fast-tracked. They married shortly afterward and remained so until she died. My brother, who is about three years younger

than me, was born prematurely after she had multiple miscarriages due to the genetic disease.

My family lived well and better than most on both sides of the family. From the outside, our homes looked beautiful. Only if a nosy neighbor peeked into the windows would they see an unattractive view. It is common for parents to argue and disagree with one another in families; there is no perfect family, of course. But disputes in our home would go too far. Arguments and fighting between my parents seem to happen every other week.

There's an ancient proverb that says every story has two sides. I believe there are three sides to this story: the mother's, the father's, and the side of the children. As the oldest child, my side of the story goes something like this— we had a Lifetime story before Lifetime became a television network. Arguments and fights were so frequent that they overshadowed the good times. The physical altercations between them could rob the room of oxygen. The most vivid memories of my childhood are of my parents' intense confrontations.

Sometimes, the worst enemy you can face is your own memory. Whenever disagreements started, I would pee on myself, especially when I heard my dad's voice getting louder. My body would tense up and lose control. Someone was about to get hurt. During those moments, I was as terrified of my stepdad as children are of the boogie man. There are so many memories of similar incidents that I could write an entire book series about them alone.

One traumatic altercation stands out to me. We were taking a family drive when my stepdad jerked the wheel without warning down a dirt road beside a corner store. I'm not sure of the store's name, but it had the best cheese biscuits. There was no doubt in my mind that something terrible was about to happen.

I knew this dirt road because one of the members of our church lived a few miles away. We got halfway up the road when my mama opened the passenger door and hurled herself out of the car. Her body rolled a few times into the ditch.

My brother and I glanced through the back window of the car and started yelling. Mama got up and slowly limped towards the store. She was covered in grass and dirt. The car began moving in reverse. It occurred to me that my stepdad might run her over. My heart pounded as I feared for my mama's life.

He swiftly turned around the car and saw that she had already reached the store. Once we arrived at the store, we pulled into the parking lot. After going into the store, my dad returned to the car with my mama. When she got in the car, I noticed that Mama's knees and elbows were bleeding. We rode home in silence, listening to the song by the Commodores called "Sail On." I'm not too fond of that song to this day. I would do anything not to have witnessed that fight. Too often, my brother and I were spectators during their disputes.

I recently spoke to my dad about our different sides of the story during a come-to-Jesus meeting. I found it hard to accept what he said since Mama wasn't there to be able to share her perspective. However, my dad's side was this: "Precious, Mamie would lie and

mismanage a lot of money. I would give her all the money from my jobs, but she would not pay the bills. Back then, we had good money. I wasn't beating her as you might think. I was scaring her."

I was glad my dad and I talked about it, but it wasn't satisfying. I felt like my dad was trying to blame my mama for everything. It is true that Mama would put our family in an unstable financial situation. But from a child's eyes, it didn't look like he was trying to scare her. I did say there are more than two sides to a story— he was beating her "a——."

Personally, I think fighting is all about being fair. As a woman with physical disabilities, my mama could not defend herself against my dad. I don't understand what kind of stronger, able-bodied person could receive any honor and respect from that. Was a healthy household too much to ask for or give to my brother and me?

The truth is that both of my parents contributed to our family's dysfunction. It was one thing for our parents to argue in front of us, but it was another thing for them to drag us into their fights. My parents' greatest mistake was to force my brother and me to

choose sides while witnessing such frightening acts of violence.

It's unfortunate that the past doesn't always remain in the past. Several years ago, while fixing my stepdad's computer, we had a big argument. We exchanged a few choice words, his voice echoing the same anger I would hear as a child. My body reacted the same way as it used to. Pee ran down the inside of my jeans.

It is very uncomfortable to talk about this. It shows though how trauma lingers even as a grown-a—— woman. The effects of unresolved trauma can manifest in various ways, including fear, anxiety, shame, grief, and unhealthy relationships. Truthfully, trauma builds self-protective walls and can become comfortable to keep, especially if it is all you know.

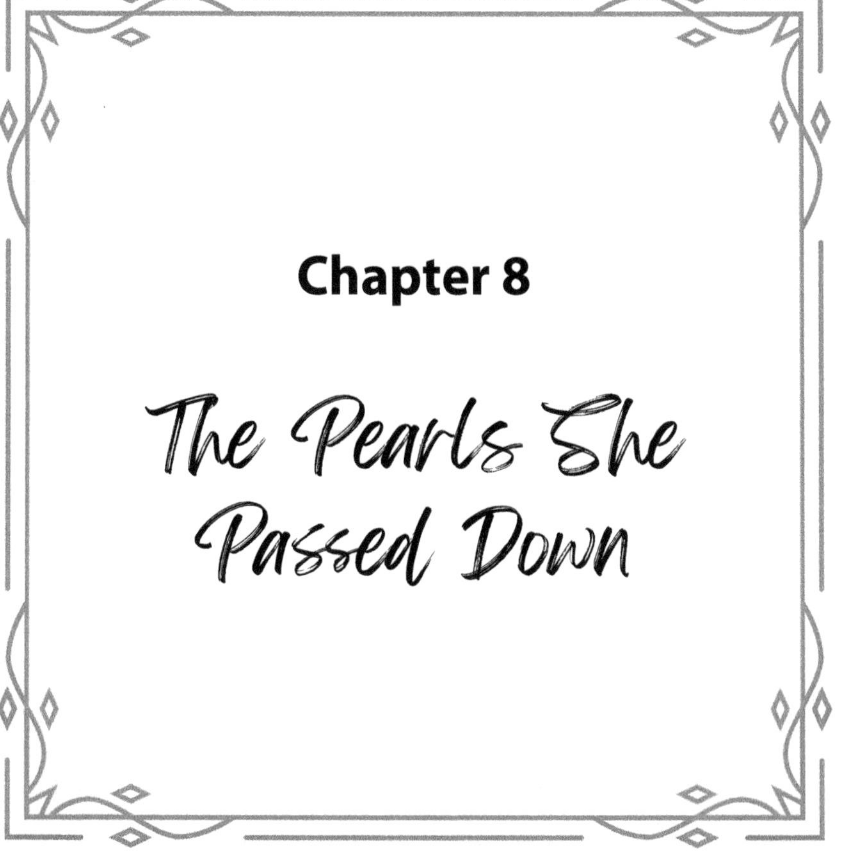

# Chapter 8

# The Pearls She Passed Down

It's quite common for people to fear becoming like their parents. The fear of becoming my mama was one of my worst nightmares. As I grew older, I saw myself becoming like her more and more. I once believed that we lived in two totally different worlds. As the genetic disease progressed in me, tumors grew and invaded my body, making our similarities more apparent.

I grew up watching Mama experience many complications resulting from NF—the good, the bad, and the ugly. She was in and out of hospitals for most of her life but always returned to us. I loved my mama, and she loved us dearly, but our relationship with each other and neurofibromatosis had never been simple. I used to try to solve the equation: My mama + me + NF =? I never could.

The more I tried to hide my feelings about trying to solve this complex equation regarding my life, the harder it became. I held my breath almost every day, anticipating something happening to me. The early death of my mama at the age of thirty-six caused me to don a specter of death like it was an everyday item of clothing. As I approached thirty-six, I just knew it would be my turn.

I felt a sense of weight being lifted from my shoulders when I passed that age. I could exhale, at least for a moment. It seems like my worries have invaded me like weeds in a garden, more since I turned forty-four. The older you get, you see age differently. I'm always in fear and rushing to get things done.

I still can see the footprints my mama left behind. I did not have the same predicament as OJ Simpson. My footsteps fit nicely into hers, while OJ's hands were too big for the gloves in his criminal case. I have learned to deal with my feelings over time and somewhat accept NF and all that comes with it.

The disease that my mama had is also afflicting me. My inherited disorder is mild, at least for now. Compared to Mama, I only have different-sized tumors and various café-au-lait discolorations covering my body. My epilepsy and a learning disability are additional accessories of NF. The relationship Mama and I had with our bodies was never good for either of us.

Mama had brownish-black café-au-lait spots covering her whole body, a deformed chest that protruded in a hump, and a

non-functional left hand. She had countless surgeries to remove tumors and participated in several experimental procedures. None of them seemed to benefit her but caused more problems.

There was one surgery where a surgeon removed an overgrown tumor, which was actually made of several tumors that hung from Mama's left arm. A skin graft from her right thigh was used to cover the area where the overgrown tumor was removed. Mama was left partially paralyzed in her left hand after the surgeon severed nerves there, resulting in her fingers curling up like a stroke victim.

I'm not fully certain what she signed or agreed to in the paperwork with the surgeon, but she never received compensation for the mistake. I recollect an instance when I over-heard the doctor tell the nurse he was going to drill two holes in my mama's skull to relieve pressure on her spine. I feared for her and wondered what would happen if the doctor screwed up again and punctured her brain.

I visited Mama a few days later after that procedure. Thick, circular metal rods extending

from her head reminded me of the bolt in Frankenstein's monster's neck; the metal rods were attached to a weighted machine. Her entire hospital stay was spent lying on her back; one wrong move would make her cringe. Over time, her condition worsened as she underwent countless procedures without success.

It was unsettling to see my body change because of neurofibromatosis. I avoided visiting a doctor for a long time until I became more responsible for my health. I did not want anything to do with medicines, procedures, and surgeries. I wasn't trying to be a doctor's guinea pig like my mama was. As my condition progressively worsened, I eventually experienced complications requiring medical care.

I find myself in this lifelong affair with NF twenty-four years later, and I am even more terrified because the tumors are growing in unexpected places. I have small tumors from head to toe and a silver dollar-sized tumor on my right forearm. I also have larger tumors on the back of my legs, so large that sometimes I have to tape them down to make them less noticeable.

Like my mama, I have been called selective nicknames throughout the years. Mama was called "Frontback of Notre Dame" since the severe scoliosis of her spinal cord curved inward, causing her chest to protrude forward into a hump. Because of the multiple hyperpigmented spots and tumors on my body, I have been called "Spot Dog." The nicknames we shared were "Monster" and "Freak."

These names were accompanied by ignorance and cruelty as well. There was a quite memorable occasion when Mama and I went to get our hair done once. As soon as we entered the beauty shop, there was a hush. The only sound I heard was hairdryers. Without receiving any greetings, my mama said, "I'd like to have my daughter and my hair done."

No one said a word. Once again, Mama repeated, "I want my daughter and my hair done."

No one replied. The ladies under the dryers and the other waiting customers were staring at this woman with blonde finger waves wearing a purple and black smock. She

was likely the owner, and the customers were waiting for her to speak.

"Come on, Precious, I think we came to a f——'n deaf beauty shop," said Mama.

I giggled. I could hear the gossip starting as soon as I shut the door. My mama drove a couple of blocks away to another beauty shop. This time she told me to stay in the car. Mama waved me into the beauty shop a few minutes later.

The second I walked into the store, I heard my favorite church song "Jesus Can Work It Out" playing in the background. As I sat down in a salon chair, a short, stout woman smiled and wrapped a smock around me. Within a few hours, we walked out of the beauty shop with our usual hairstyles, me with braids and my mama with her Jheri curl.

Years later, I had something similar happen at a massage parlor, but with speaking people. Soft music filled the massage parlor, and a red-haired woman pointed me to a room along with some directions.

I removed my clothes in a slightly dim room and lay down on a cold massage table. A few seconds later, the red-haired woman began

rubbing my body with her hands. I felt the flat sheet lift off me, then fall back on me. The red-haired woman bolted out of the room. I raised my head to see what was going on.

"Is everything okay?" I called out.

As the door closed, I could only get a glimpse of her red ponytail. I wrapped the white sheet around myself and reached for my purple cell phone next to the massage table. I told myself she had ten minutes to get back, but I waited thirty minutes trying to show grace. Angry, I put on my clothes again and left the room.

One of the workers began walking in my direction, turned around, then walked away. I approached the glass window of the front office and began tapping the countertop bell. After several taps, no one answered. I could see a worker hiding in the corner through a mirror hanging in the office. My taps on the bell were followed by banging on the glass, and soon three ladies appeared.

"What's going on?" I asked as one particularly brave lady pulled back the glass. She stepped back, clutching the collar of her pink blouse with her fingers, and said nothing. My

first thought was that I could help her choke herself.

"We do not feel comfortable serving you," she said. I took a deep breath and requested my money back.

"There are no refunds," she said, "However, we can give you a gift card."

"What in the h—— will I do with a gift card?" I replied, trembling.

"Maybe you can give it to someone as a gift," she offered. I walked away, trying to keep the Hulk out. She quickly closed and locked the window.

Once I was in my Mazda, I turned the radio to the highest possible volume. My phone began ringing after about ten miles of driving. I did not recognize the number, so I let the phone go to voicemail. Reaching the front of my apartment complex, I listened to the voicemail.

"Ms. Nobles, this is a manager from the massage shop. We will send you a refund to the address you provided on the client information sheet."

Shaking my head, I looked at the sky and asked God, "Why me?"

Mama was the strongest person I have ever known. She had a backbone made from steel and a heart made of gold. She continued to love no matter what she was experiencing behind closed doors and on the streets. Those who knew my mama know she was sweet like chocolate candy. She would give her last to anyone without asking for anything in return, especially to family and friends. I am the same way.

Mama was an over-giver, but sometimes her gifts were not out of generosity. They were out of a buried need. Her giving was also unbalanced; she would only receive a fraction of what she gave. It is not that giving is a bad thing, far from it. Mama gave so much to others that it often put our immediate family in dire financial situations, which caused countless fights with my dad. The aftermath was unpaid utility bills, the loss of several houses, cars, and our stability. Our income came from Dad's drywall hustles, and my mama received disability for herself, my brother, and me.

As seen earlier, I found myself giving away my money, time, and body. You name it, I have given it. I gave so much that I did not have

enough of anything for myself. I believe the over-giving of my mama and I goes beyond just giving to others. We obtained our relationships by over-giving to be accepted and receive love.

While my mama was generous, she was also deceitful and conniving. I doubt she intended to harm anyone. I think she would do anything to avoid abandonment, even if it demonstrated a lack of character. She would, for example, write a bad check to buy a gift and lie about writing the check.

Although I am a Doctor of Philosophy, not a medical doctor, I believe Mama suffered from an undiagnosed mental issue. She always seemed different than the other mothers I knew. She was suffering from something that I didn't understand. Upon connecting some dots in the family history, I discovered that mental illness and depression were also prevalent on both sides of Mama's family.

The apple didn't fall too far from the tree. At various times in my life, I lacked character as well. Before I met Jesus, I could be as equally conniving as my mama. Even though I couldn't understand exactly what she was going

through, I've been diagnosed and treated for anxiety, chronic depression, borderline personality disorder, and PTSD.

Mama and I were both told we weren't good enough somewhere along the way. The belief that we weren't good enough drove our life choices. Every action we took was motivated by proving our worth. We were haunted by it. In retrospect, my inner need to be accepted by others proved to be an illusion. What I received for my efforts was only a temporary demonstration of love and care.

I have always felt uncomfortable in my own skin throughout my life, regardless of the period. I was unwilling to accept the genetic disorder of neurofibromatosis and looked for someone to blame for it. Like a connect-the-dots puzzle, I linked the disease and everything I experienced from it to my mama. Within my immature logical mind, she was to blame for this degenerative affliction and for passing it down to my brother and me.

I felt Mama was a little selfish. This condition did not choose us, but she chose our fate. She knew the path of NF better than anyone else and the burden it carried all too

well. I did not think even God could be left off the hook, why He would choose to heal some and not others. I know no one is to blame, perhaps only Adam and Eve. Regardless, my mama endured a lot given the circumstances, and did her best.

I have asked myself why Mama would want this condition for my brother and me. I don't think she was concerned about the disease. My brother and I may have been crucial to her sense of love and worth. What Mama didn't receive; she gave to us— that's what I call love. The love I was searching for was like that of Mary J. Blige. Right in front of me was real love, my mama.

With age, I have come to understand what Mama had tried to do for me, my family, and others throughout her life. My mama, Mamie Ann Nobles Valentine, did not know her worth until it was too late. That outcome will not be the same for me. I desire to move to the next level in all aspects of my life, yet something keeps getting my way.

# Chapter 9

## Tailored Clothes

I have never been able to determine what it is that makes a person whole or how a person can feel whole alone. I ponder whether different types of relationships or material things can fill emptiness and how that idea resonates with others. There has never been a time when I have ever felt whole. My wholeness has always been based on my relationships with others as well as my academic achievements. However, I am unable to pinpoint when this lack of wholeness began.

One connection that stands out in my mind quite vividly is a day that has plagued and followed me my entire life. A teacher and I were in the classroom discussing my plans after high school when I shared that I wanted to become a lawyer or teacher.

The teacher laughed, "Radscheda, you're smarter than your classmates but not smart enough for college." I had been relegated to a special classroom with all different types of special needs students. According to her, I would not be able to comprehend college material quickly enough, and my medical

disorders along with my learning disability would burden instructors.

After a pause she chided, "Radscheda, get college out of your head! You will be a great worker at any fast-food chain. It would be best for you to work somewhere that does not require much thinking and can overlook your limitations. I researched your condition a little bit; don't expect much in your life. Before leaving this class, I will ensure that you are the best worker at McDonald's, Burger King, or any restaurant you decide to work at."

She handed me the fake cash register; then, we began roleplaying life assignments. Her position of authority as my teacher caused me not to question her judgment. I couldn't think of any reasons why she would lead me astray.

I agreed with her assessment. I have been a slow learner. This sentiment has been expressed by others about my learning abilities as well. Even now, as a professor with a doctorate and an academic career spanning fifteen years, I am still held to lower standards and expectations.

While working at Burger King a few years later, I met that teacher again. That day, several crew members had called in sick. Only the manager, one sandwich maker, and I were at the restaurant during rush hour. As I glanced down the line of hungry people, I recognized my dream-crushing teacher from high school. I instantly flashbacked to sitting at my desk again, remembering our conversation.

As I stood in front of that cash register, her hypothesis about me was confirmed. She was beaming from ear to ear as she reached the cash register, "Radscheda, you worked the cash register, and I didn't have to wait at all!" she said, "I knew you would make a good fast-food worker."

I rolled my eyes and asked, "How can I help you today?"

Don't get me wrong; there is nothing wrong with working at a fast-food place. Even though the money is still green, I wouldn't like to work there every day of my life. The irony of the situation was that the teacher thought she had helped me out. If only she knew how her words crushed what little confidence I had. She appears to be a trending type of

teacher all over the world. I've heard motivational speakers and overcomers mention other people like her.

We live in an unpredictable world. Every single person will experience or encounter challenges in life. It is not uncommon for lives to spiral out of control when faced with challenges. I felt like my life was spiraling out of control, and I could never catch a break. I was battling a relentless medical condition and became motherless, a high school dropout, homeless, and many other things I regret. Yet those same challenges gave me the strength to fight for myself later in life.

In order to succeed and buck against the system, I developed the tools I needed to succeed and win. Those tools allowed me to defy statistics and other people's expectations. The underdog stories I've read have advised me to "focus on what you can do, not on what you can't."

At this stage of my life, I no longer wanted to follow any rules or play a role. Despite the odds and everything that has gone wrong in my life, I have always felt like an underdog, someone like Rocky Balboa. I simply couldn't release all the turmoil in my life.

I didn't stay at Burger King; I just stopped by. There were still a number of hardships I had to overcome before seeing the light at the end of the tunnel. The obstacles and setbacks I have experienced in my career have always been a point of contention for me. My GED (Graduate Equivalency Degree) was obtained several years later while I was homeless. With the GED, I became more employable and was able to enroll in a community college.

I surprised myself by doing well in community college. I then transferred to Shaw University from the local community college. I completed my bachelor's degree with honors within three years. Although I was still working at low-paying jobs such as restaurants and stores, I had dreams for the first time in my life.

I ran into the dream-crushing teacher again one day in the hallway of my high school. When she saw me in the hall, she asked, "Do you have a kid here?"

I pointed to my classroom door and replied, "No, I work here."

She frowned, walked into her classroom, and shut the door. My younger self wanted

to express how I felt about her advice all those years ago, but a little voice inside kept me from doing so. Those experiences taught me that you need to allow some people to speak and then show them. The best part is that you will never have to say "I told you so" since they will already know.

Next, I enrolled in a master's program. I must admit that this was not an easy process for me. At this stage, I thought about all of my dream-crushing teachers again. My professors in the master's program were excellent, but there weren't enough resources for a student like me, a student with learning disorders and disabilities.

My biggest challenge at this level was figuring out how I learned. For the first time in my life, I thought about the possibility that I could be smart enough, but I would have to restack my deck to get the outcome I wanted.

It became more important to me at that time of my life to act on the advice to focus on what I could do well rather than on what I could not do well. It was time for me to change my mindset. I would have to learn how to play all my cards, even those I didn't want to play.

This was not an easy task; I had to work even harder and work through all my weaknesses. There were times when this was exhausting. No matter what, I felt I had to put in the effort. I had always been a backseat rider when it came to my education. People would often consign me to a role or place of their preference, and I would just accept that as my assignment.

I finally decided to take charge of my educational plans myself and found a way to succeed. My master's degree was also earned with honors. In the days leading up to my graduate degree ceremony, I was offered an instructor position at a university, which I accepted.

I became passionate about teaching students. I had no qualms about sharing where I came from or who I was and wasn't with anyone, whether they were students or colleagues. This was difficult because I was not the poster child for the professorial image or typical professor.

I was reminded of my junior high days when there were the pretty girls and then me. Now it was the professors, and I did not

receive the same respect as other colleagues. Regardless, I have found a place in academics and teaching with my uniqueness.

To go to the next level, I had to pass the GRE in order to be considered for a doctorate program. I never did well on tests, no matter how hard I studied. I was able to obtain learning accommodations now that I was in control of my education, like the allowance of extra time while taking the GRE. Although I was given more time on the GRE test, I still did not score well. Undiscouraged, I decided to rely on my history of good grades to apply to several Ph.D. programs. Despite several rejections, I received an opportunity at Howard University.

In terms of spirituality, working towards a doctorate was analogous to the battle between David and Goliath, or perhaps even the boxing match between Rocky and the Russian Ivan Drago. Even though the doctoral program was arduous, dealing with ignorant people was even more difficult. I had to arrange accommodations with various professors, for example. It was a nightmare.

I recollect presenting my learning accommodation to a professor. She glanced at the

requirements and asked, "Do you expect accommodations at this level?" I assume you know that this is a Ph.D. level?"

My response was, "Yes, and yes."

"Let's try my way first, and if that doesn't work, let's try these accommodations," she asserted.

"Okay," I said and walked away.

Her way did not work for me, and she let me use my requested time extension for the next exam. I did well, but she stated that she didn't respect me for using it at the doctorate level.

Issues like these continued, as well as other petty power struggles that happened in different classes. I'd taken many punches in my life, and I'd been able to get back up. It became apparent that the doctoral process would not be any different.

The moment I held my Ph.D. degree in my hands, a tear rolled down my cheek. It dawned on me that I had wanted all my academic achievements for the wrong reasons. In my heart, I sincerely hoped they would prove everyone wrong and shut up the naysayers.

I wanted to cover up all the undesirable things about myself as well. I had been a high school dropout and side chick and had experienced homelessness, neurofibromatosis, and grief. There was also the heartache I caused my mama and others.

If I'm honest with myself, I used these achievements to make myself whole. It did not take long for me to discover my degrees could not and would not change anything. It didn't make me a better person or make people respect me more because I was highly educated.

No person or thing can make us whole. Unfortunately, we often believe it can. I spent many years letting people steal my moments that were not theirs to take. It's essential to learn not just to celebrate the accomplishment but also the process.

# Chapter 10

## The Dressing Room

Awkward situations in a dressing room, like accidentally ripping an outfit or getting stuck in one while trying it on, are a part of the human experience. Or perhaps it's just me who's done that. I'm pretty confident though, that my personal awkward dressing room experiences could top the craziest of them all.

I live a life no differently than others. Like many people, I enjoy going out to eat, going on dates, and shopping. For me, outings always end in a twist. A visit to a clothing store comes to mind. I had to go to a store to buy a dress for my graduate school's gala.

I walked straight to the sale racks without hesitation. At the end of the last rack of dresses, I spotted a tight black skirt with gold sequins between a section of tightly packed dresses. There was an additional 30 percent off tag on the price tag. The price was right, but I had a dilemma. My concern was whether the tumors would appear like lumps through the form-fitting dress.

My next move was to go to the dressing room. A dressing room attendant took a bouncer-like stance and stared at the

half-dollar-sized tumor on my right arm before scanning my entire body. She then told me I wasn't allowed in the fitting room.

With an overdue manicure, she picked up the receiver from the phone with multiple lines hanging on the wall and pressed the number three. She held the phone close to her lips outlined in black and said, "I need a manager to come to the dressing room."

A man wearing a name tag labeled manager appeared. The manager and the sales associate eyed me as they huddled for a few minutes. I wondered if I was about to get bounced out of the dressing room. It wouldn't be the first time.

My mind was whirling with thoughts. Did my disease strike again? Maybe I should have worn a long-sleeved shirt or jacket. I was caught off guard when the manager approached and said, "I am sorry, ma'am. Please go ahead to the dressing room."

I was feeling vulnerable when I went to try on the dress. I felt even worse once the dress was not "right and tight." So, I headed out of the fitting room and hung the dress on the return clothes rack. The sales associate

with the outlined black lips grabbed the dress and forcefully began shaking it before I could step away.

My guess was that she thought I left some residue of tumors and spots behind. Perhaps, they would fall from the dress by her shaking it. Shaking my head, I began to walk away again. Immediately, she picked up the phone and called another department, "Do you have any Lysol? This woman over here with all these bumps tried on a dress; I have no idea what they are."

I walked back toward her. "Let me try on the dress again; maybe some more tumors will fall off. You are so worried about my tumors; some people have tried on clothes they haven't washed their a——. "

She stared at me in shock as I walked away. While I wiped away tears, I wondered to myself, *D——, can I get a break? God, where are you?*

Situations like that still happen so frequently that my self-esteem sometimes takes a hit, making me feel less than human. The irony of that instance was that she started greeting me when I visited the store again.

We are sometimes placed in situations, not for ourselves but to change someone else.

One dressing room incident, however, would forever change me. My dissertation defense was approaching, so I needed to buy a blouse to go with a pinstripe suit. My goal was to look as professional as possible because I was about to become Dr. Nobles. I was determined not to let anything or anyone stand in my way, not even the dressing room. I've always thought Dr. Radscheda has a nice ring to it.

This dressing room was different from the others because it seemed self-serve, or perhaps there was a staff shortage that day. After I stepped into the third dressing room, I pulled a thick blue curtain with a white border behind me.

I slipped my shirt over my head, replacing it with a long white blouse. Even though my tumors could be seen through the blouse, I loved it. A black undershirt and a suit jacket could easily solve that problem.

While crushing over myself in the full-length mirror, I noticed someone eyeballing me between the three-inch gap in the curtain.

I felt my heart pounding rapidly, and I was scared. Uncertain of what was about to happen, I quickly glanced into my purse for any weapon I could use.

The first things I noticed were a couple of open ink pens in my purse, a nail file with a sharp tip, and a fork I had used for lunch earlier. I have watched too many scary movies to become a victim; it was not my intention to become a victim that day.

At first, I thought the fork would be the ideal weapon, but then I remembered the mace at the bottom of my bag. I slowly slipped my T-shirt over my head after palming the mace. Never once did I blink or look away from the mirror.

Turning around, I quickly whipped the curtain to the right. In front of me was a tiny woman standing behind the dusty curtain. She had an afro with a Cruella de Vil gray stripe in the front and was clutching clothes in her hand. It was just a little old lady, but everyone could be a suspect, so I held onto the mace tightly.

"Can I help you?" I asked her. I guess the woman was afraid of what I might do or

maybe was even embarrassed because she seemed hesitant to say anything.

"Why are you staring in my dressing room?" I questioned.

"I am sorry," she said trembling, "I have never seen anything like those bumps."

DMX's "Y'all Gon' Make Me Lose My Mind" ran thematically through my mind. I paused for a moment. I swear God's grace overcame me when I heard a new song filter through called, "Break Every Chain," by Tasha Cobbs Leonard. It goes something like this, "There is power in the name of Jesus to break every chain, break every chain, break every chain."

I breathed deeply. Then, I told the old lady I had "Neurofibromatosis." But after explaining the condition to her, she still stood in front of me inside the dressing room. Although I held the love of God in my heart, I still brushed past her in a DMX fashion to show her that I was the boss.

I then proceeded to the cash register to purchase my blouse. DMX's song was playing in my head, and Tasha Cobbs Leonard's song was playing in my heart simultaneously. It was the song in my heart that won.

It crossed my mind to tell the cashier, speak with a manager, or even call the police about what happened in the dressing room.

But I stayed true to myself for the first time in my life. Laughter filled my belly as I walked away with my head high. It reminded me of my speeding rocket days when I won that award, and everyone in class crowded around me. I didn't need that same validation this time; instead, I gave it to myself.

That day in the dressing room, God intervened. I learned at that moment that the only person that could save me was myself, God too. My biggest challenge was letting go of my pain and forgiving, even if it felt impossible.

Two thoughts came to mind as well. First, I had stood up to neurofibromatosis, insecurity, and shame. I realized that ignorance will always play a significant role in my life and even pain, but I must remain positive and not let these events define me. Second, this woman stopped in her tracks to admire my accessories of neurofibromatosis, and I educated her.

It's common for people to wear watches, cufflinks, pearl earrings, necklaces, heels, bracelets, or anything that enhances an

outfit. It is, however, impossible to remove certain accessories. Some accessories we get to choose to wear, and some we don't. My mama's deformity and life experiences were irremovable accessories that accentuated her "life outfit."

Like my mama, trauma, my genetic disorder, mental illness, and even my learning disability are my irremovable accessories. However, they complement my "Dr. Radscheda Nobles" outfit. As I work to accept myself and love these accessories, I have decided to wear them the same way I wear pearls.

I have experienced moments of severe brokenness in my life, allowing people to take advantage of my brokenness for their benefit. As I've mentioned before, the truth is that trauma and grief are not just in your head. I learned from my mama's death that pain has a way of making us feel stuck. Holding onto pain does not fix anything in life. Time heals, yet healing has its own timeline.

I spent most of my life trying to fill empty spaces with everything possible, only to find that nothing is likely to fill these spots—only God can. The past is a done deal. We cannot

change it. I have lived almost my whole life without my mama, and I will always be a little broken without her. Nowadays, I often dream about us being together. Within these dreams, it's as if she never died, and we're getting along well. Maybe this is just the way I'm currently coping in this season.

Do not make the same mistake I did and confuse pivotal life transitions with spiritual warfare. I endured this intense internal battle between my mind, body, and soul that weighed upon me with perpetual pressure as I struggled to survive my pain. I honestly thought the bondage of my destructive behavioral habits and patterns, my trauma, grief, and unforeseen events in my life were there to harm and destroy me. But that was not the case.

It was difficult to find clarity when I was in a transitional phase— the pain-built wall around me blinded me. No one wants to struggle, but our lives are tested by hardships, and we can grow during these times. God can take a broken life and resurrect it to life with a purpose.

There are times when God allows us to go through things. Those things are not in place to hurt or damage us but to prepare us. Just because we have been broken does not mean we cannot be repaired. It takes time to overcome past trauma or pain. The power of God, however, can make anything beautiful.

In the healing process, a different story can be told— one that you can be proud of. I am proud of my story and my testimony. I am only a vessel and still a work in progress. Don't forget— healing does not follow a timeline.

**...To be continued**

Close the book and flip to the gold cover to read Part II of my story …

Close the book and flip to the black cover to read Part I of my story…